Cambridge English Readers

Level 2

Series editor: Philip Prowse

D0040585

The Man from Nowhere

Bernard Smith

CAMBRIDGE
UNIVERSITY PRESS

CAMBRIDGE
UNIVERSITY PRESS

University Printing House, Cambridge CB2 8BS, United Kingdom

Cambridge University Press is part of the University of Cambridge.

It furthers the University's mission by disseminating knowledge in the pursuit of education, learning and research at the highest international levels of excellence.

www.cambridge.org
Information on this title: www.cambridge.org/9780521783613

© Cambridge University Press 2001

This publication is in copyright. Subject to statutory exception and to the provisions of relevant collective licensing agreements, no reproduction of any part may take place without the written permission of Cambridge University Press.

First published 2001
Reprinted 2015

Printed in the United Kingdom by Hobbs the Printers Ltd

A catalogue record for this publication is available from the British Library

ISBN 978-0-521-78361-3 Paperback

Cambridge University Press has no responsibility for the persistence or accuracy of URLs for external or third-party internet websites referred to in this publication, and does not guarantee that any content on such websites is, or will remain, accurate or appropriate. Information regarding prices, travel timetables and other factual information given in this work is correct at the time of first printing but Cambridge University Press does not guarantee the accuracy of such information thereafter.

Illustrations by Debbie Hinks

Contents

Characters

A pilot and his wife and son
Inspector Ibrahim
Nurse Imelda
Dr Singh

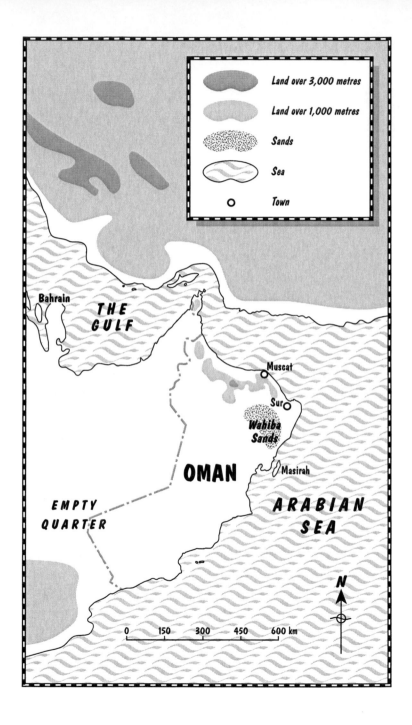

Land over 3,000 metres

Land over 1,000 metres

Sands

Sea

Town

Bahrain

THE GULF

Muscat

Sur

Wahiba Sands

OMAN

Masirah

EMPTY QUARTER

ARABIAN SEA

N

0   150   300   450   600 km

Chapter 1 *Wahiba*

The Wahiba Sands – a soft sand desert in north east Oman. Two hundred kilometres from north to south; a hundred from east to west. Long dunes run north to south, long lines of sand, always changing, always moving in the wind.

On its west side, Wahiba is a long wall of red sand, fifty or sixty metres high. It runs slowly down on to the empty desert, which is the centre of Oman. Hard, stony and flat as a table, this desert is the eastern side of the great *rub' al-khali*, the Empty Quarter.

In the east, the dunes of sand run down on to long, empty beaches. Crabs and seabirds live there by day, and green turtles often come out of the sea to lay their eggs by night. After the beaches, there is only the deep blue-green water of the Arabian Sea for fifteen hundred kilometres to Gujarat in northern India.

The sands of Wahiba are empty and quiet. There is no sound. Nothing bigger than a lizard can live in the great sea of soft, red-gold sand; nothing bigger than marram grass can grow there. You hear nothing but the blood in your ears, and the hot dry air going in and out of your mouth.

To walk in the soft sand is difficult. It pulls your feet as you walk. Your legs soon hurt and you get tired very quickly. To move at all is hard work.

And, of course, in the day the hot sun is always there.

The air is hot, the sand is hot. There is nowhere you can go away from the sun, no tree as far as you can see.

In the sky above the blue-green Indian Ocean, a small plane is coming from the east. Red and white, two engines, the only sound in the quiet sky.

Chapter 2   *Red snow*

'Are you OK? Would you like some coffee?'

The man looked back and smiled.

'Good idea,' he said. 'I'm feeling all right, but coffee would be good.'

The woman came and sat in the seat next to the man. She had two cups of coffee in her hand.

'Where are we?' she asked, looking out at the clear blue sky outside the plane.

'Can you see that thin brown line where the sky meets the sea?' said the man. 'Well, that's the coast of Oman. We're going north now along the coast.'

'That's good,' said the woman, giving the man a cup. 'When do you think we'll get to Tehran?'

'How's Andy?' asked the man.

'He's fine. He's asleep on the back seat. We got up very early this morning. He was very tired.'

'Good,' said the man. 'I want to talk to you and I don't want Andy to hear.'

'Is there a problem?' asked the woman.

'Not really. I've just talked to our friend Parvis in Tehran on the radio. He says the weather in Tehran is terrible. It's not a good time to go there.'

'Oh dear, and I wanted to see it,' said the woman.

'We can go next year, when the weather's better,' said the man. 'I told Parvis we won't come this time. It's no good if the weather is wet and cold.'

'What do we want to do then? Are we going straight home?' asked the woman.

'No,' said the man. 'We're free until next Wednesday and we haven't had a holiday together for a long time. I thought we could go to Bahrain tonight. We could see our friends Neil and Rosie there. Then I thought we could go to Paris for a few days. It's Andy's birthday on Saturday. We could go to EuroDisney in Paris with him.'

'Why not? Good idea,' said the woman. 'We won't tell Andy until we get there. It'll be a nice surprise for him.'

'OK. I'll call Bahrain on the radio and tell them we're coming. I talked to the people on Masirah a few minutes ago. We're OK to fly north along the coast. I'll radio Bahrain when I've had my coffee.'

The woman put her face against the plane window and half closed her eyes. There was nothing but clear blue sky and deep green-blue sea. Then she saw the thin line of sandy brown to the left.

'That's the coast of Oman, you say,' she said.

The man looked to the left. The brown sandy line of the desert coast of Oman was now quite clear.

'That's the Wahiba Sands,' he said. 'I don't think you've ever seen it. It's beautiful. It's a great soft sand desert. I was there about ten years ago when I worked in Oman.'

The man turned the plane to the west and took it slowly down.

'We're too high to see it well,' he said. 'I'll take us down to about three hundred metres. Then you can see the coast and the dunes.'

The plane flew low over the coast, a wide empty beach, a few small houses next to the sea. Then only the long gold lines of the dunes.

'Beautiful!' said the woman. 'You're right. So clean. So empty. I've never seen anything like it. But don't go too far. Turn round now.'

'OK,' said the man, and the small plane turned slowly in the hot clean air.

The woman put some more coffee into the man's cup. The man turned in his seat and took the cup.

Later he remembered seeing the cup full of coffee in his hand, brown and hot. Then everything began to happen very slowly.

First there was a light to his left – a quick, white light. And a noise, first a bang, then a loud noise that went on and on.

Something hit his face, hard, on the left side between his left eye and his ear. Then, suddenly, he was half sitting and half lying on the floor of the plane. The noise was terrible. He could not think. He could not move.

The air in the plane was full of snow, white and flying about slowly in the air. Then the snow was red – red snow everywhere in the air.

The woman looked slowly down at him. Her face and body were red with the thick snow. Her eyes and mouth were wide open but he could not hear anything.

'That's blood on her face,' he thought. 'Why is there blood on her face? And she is shouting at me, but I can't hear what she is saying. I can't hear anything over the terrible noise.'

There was another noise now, *Beep! Beep! Beep!* Like a car. He knew it meant danger of some kind, but he could not think.

From the floor of the plane he looked up. The woman was flying the plane, her eyes and mouth wide open and her face red with blood.

'That's wrong,' he thought. 'She doesn't know how to fly a plane. She can't do it.'

Then he was suddenly in the air. He felt his body fly up and hit something hard. Then everything was black.

Chapter 3 *Crash*

Hot . . . red light . . . white light . . . close your eyes . . . it hurts. Headache, terrible headache . . . pain everywhere . . . a voice calling his name . . . again and again.

The man opened his eyes slowly. A boy's face . . . Andy. Hot sun on his face. White light and pain in his eyes.

'Where . . . what?' he said.

'Dad,' Andy said. 'Wake up. I need you.'

The man tried to move but his body was full of pain. He could not move his head. He moved his eyes and looked about slowly. All around there was red sand, soft red sand. Above his head was something long and red against the blue sky. Long and red. He knew what it was. The wing of the plane. This was all wrong.

'Your mother . . .' he said.

'She's all right,' said his son. 'She's hurt her foot, but it's not bad.'

The man looked at the wing of the plane above him. Now he knew why it was wrong. It was the top of the wing which was red. Below it was white.

He moved to sit up. His head hurt like fire but he could see more. A wing against a clear blue sky. A window half under the soft red sand.

'What happened, Andy?' he asked. 'Do you know?'

The boy shook his head.

'I was asleep in the back. Next thing I knew we were here in the sand. Lucky I had my seat belt on. The plane's upside down. The front is all broken and under the sand. Mum and me pulled you out. We thought the plane could catch fire. But it's OK. Mum's lying here behind you. She's hurt her foot. I've got all the suitcases and the food and drinks out of the plane. They're over there under the wing.'

The man turned. The woman was sitting on the sand.

Her face and clothes were thick with dry blood. Her teeth were very white as she smiled.

'I know it looks terrible,' she said quickly. 'But it's not my blood, and it's not yours. So don't be afraid. I think we hit some birds. One of them, maybe more, came through the plane window and there were blood and feathers everywhere. A big piece of the window hit you on the side of the head. You were unconscious for a time and I couldn't fly the plane. We came down in these sand dunes. We're all lucky to be alive.'

'What happened to your foot?' asked the man.

'I don't know. It's my ankle. I think it could be broken. It really hurts. I can't walk on it.'

'Is the radio still working, do you think?'

'Not a hope. The front of the plane is in pieces and under a metre of sand.'

The man looked at the watch on his wrist. It was still working all right.

'Two fifteen in the afternoon,' he said. 'The hottest time of the day. We must stay here out of the sun until the sun goes down a little. Let's see what food and water we have. We could be here for some time.'

*   *   *

By four o'clock the sun was not so high in the sky and it was not so hot.

The man was feeling better. His head still hurt but he could move about. The woman's ankle hurt a lot and she could not move.

They had some drinks from the plane and some food,

cake and biscuits, but not enough even for two days in the hot dry air of the desert.

The man and his wife spoke quietly. They did not want the boy to hear.

'No-one knows we are here. I didn't radio Bahrain. No-one will start to look for us for three or four days,' said the man. 'And really, we have very little food and water.'

'We should stay with the plane,' said the woman. 'Make a fire, smoke. Someone will see us.'

'There is nothing here to make a fire with, no wood, nothing but sand. And there are no people anywhere near here, no roads, no villages. But we must be near the coast. I was turning back to the coast when we hit the birds. If I walk east, I must come to the sea in a few kilometres. There are people on the coast. I'll find someone who can help.'

'What if you get lost?' said the woman.

'I'll keep the sun on my back,' said the man. 'Then I must be going east towards the sea. I'll take one bottle of water. Keep the rest. Use it slowly and carefully. I'll be back in a day or two at the most.'

Chapter 4 *The beach*

Now it is almost six o'clock. The sun, big and red, is going down over the long dunes of the Wahiba Sands. Something is moving in the great red-gold sea. There is a long line of footprints in the sand. A man is walking slowly, up the dunes and down the other side. He is not wearing a shirt. The sun is on his back, which is burnt red.

He cannot see, he cannot think. He is putting one foot in front of the other in his sleep. He does not know where he is or who he is. He only knows that he must keep moving. Keep putting one foot in front of the other. He must keep the sun on his back. Keep moving, or die.

Suddenly, he feels that the sand is different. It is harder, easier. His feet are suddenly light and free and he falls on his face. A strange feeling – like cold hands on his face and here and there on his hot, dry body. It is all too difficult to think about. He knows he has fallen and that he cannot get up again. He gives up at last and all thinking stops.

*　　*　　*

Along the eastern coast of Oman, where the Wahiba Sands meet the sea, there are a few, very few, very small villages. There, a few people live by fishing and keeping animals.

Near one of these villages a small boy was running along the low sand dunes next to the beach. He was looking for some of his father's goats, which had walked off in the afternoon. He wanted to find them and take them back to the village before the sun went down and it was dark. Already the sun was behind the sand dunes. Their tops were a long gold line against the deep blue of the sky; their sides were changing from brown to purple.

Suddenly, the boy saw something on the sand, half in the sea. He came nearer. It was a man, lying on his face in the wet sand where the small waves washed the beach. He was not wearing clothes like the people of the village. He was wearing trousers like the women wear, and no shirt. His shoulders, arms and back were all red and burnt.

The boy came closer. The man did not move at all. The

boy ran back to the village as fast as he could. He called to his father.

'There's a dead *khawaja* on the beach,' he said. *Khawaja* was their word for foreigner.

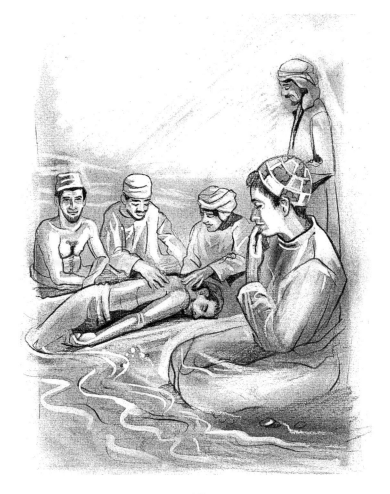

Chapter 5   *Khawaja*

The boy's father ran to the head man of the village.

'The boy says there is a dead *khawaja* on the beach,' he said.

Four men from the village ran with the boy to where the man was lying on the wet sand.

The boy's father turned the man over on his back. There was wet sand on his face and in his dark hair.

The head man put his hand on the man's neck.

'Not dead,' he said. 'He's still alive. We must take him back to the village quickly.'

The four men carried him to the village and put him in the head man's house. They put him on the floor in a dark room and washed him with cold water. They washed the sand from his face.

The head man went to a box in his house. In it was a radio telephone. He made a call, the first call that year.

A police helicopter came with a doctor from the town of Sur, two hundred kilometres to the north. They looked at the man. He was still alive, but not moving.

'We must get him to the hospital in Muscat,' said the doctor. 'This man is very ill. I can't do anything for him here.'

The helicopter took the man to the hospital in the capital city. There they took off his dirty clothes, washed him, and put him in a clean bed.

There was a plastic bag of water and drugs over the bed

and it ran slowly into the man's arm. The man had a cut on one side of his head, a bad cut, and a small cut on his face between his left eye and his ear. Nothing else, only where his back and face were burnt from the sun.

A nurse sat next to his bed all night. The man did not wake up. Sometimes his legs moved in the bed. He was walking in his sleep. Sometimes he made a low noise, like an animal. He was talking in his sleep. But the nurse could not understand what he said.

Chapter 6 *Coma*

A day went by and still the man did not move or open his eyes. The nurse by the man's bed on the second morning was from the Philippines. Her name was Imelda. She sat and watched the sleeping man. Sometimes he moved his legs or arms a little, sometimes he made a low sound. She thought perhaps he would soon wake up, and watched him carefully.

Suddenly, the man's head moved from side to side. His lips moved.

'Morphia,' he said quietly.

Imelda put her ear near to the man's mouth.

'Morphia,' he said again. 'Red snow.'

Imelda spoke to him quietly. But the man did not speak or move again.

Imelda went to the door to call Dr Singh. She wanted to tell him the man was talking. But at that moment the doctor came into the room. There was a police inspector with him.

'This is Nurse Imelda,' said the doctor to the inspector. 'She is one of the nurses who are looking after the man here, our man from nowhere. This is Inspector Ibrahim, Imelda, of the Royal Oman Police. He has come to help us find out who this man is.'

Imelda looked at the inspector. He was quite small, with grey hair and a small grey moustache.

'The man said something a few moments ago,' she said.

'I think he said "Morphia", and then something like "red snow". He was speaking in English, but I'm not sure what he said.'

'Morphia?' said the inspector. 'Is he asking for morphia or morphine, do you think? Is his head or his back hurting him?'

'I don't think so,' said the doctor. 'He has been in a coma since he came here. When you are in a coma, a very deep sleep, you don't usually feel anything. We have given him some drugs to help him. You can see there is a cut on his head, but there is nothing broken.

'It's probably nothing important – something, some words in his head. But if he is saying something, that's a good thing. Perhaps he'll wake up soon and we can find out who he is.'

Dr Singh and the inspector stood for a few moments looking at the man in the bed, but he did not move again or make any sound.

Then the inspector said, 'They told me at my office this morning that some fishermen found him on the beach north of Masirah Island late in the afternoon two days ago. He came here in a helicopter in the night, and has not moved or spoken a word until now. And nobody knows who he is or where he came from.'

'That's right,' said the doctor. 'We have no idea. We are waiting for the poor man to wake up.'

'What else can you tell me about him, then?' asked the inspector. 'There must be something. He has been here for a day and a half now.'

Dr Singh looked at his papers.

'Not a lot, I'm afraid,' he said. 'He's about thirty-five to forty years old. He's one metre 57 tall and weighs about 70 kilos. As you can see, he has brown eyes, short dark hair, a small moustache and a short beard. I don't think he's Omani. He could be Lebanese or Syrian, or he could be from any country round the Mediterranean, really. Of course, he could also be American or British. It's very hard to say.'

'What about his clothes? What was in his pockets? Things like that,' asked the inspector.

'When they found him he was wearing only some dirty white trousers. They were white jeans, made in America. Also blue shorts, blue socks and some brown boots. They're all in a plastic bag next to the bed there, if you want to look at them. But there is no name on any of them, I'm afraid. And there was nothing in the pockets, nothing at all. And he wasn't wearing a shirt of any kind, which is very strange.'

'How is he?' asked the inspector. 'Is he badly hurt? What about the cut on his head?'

'He has a cut to the left side of his head, above the ear. Quite a bad one. It was done about two or three days ago. Then he has another cut on his face. You can see it near his left eye. Not so bad as the one on his head, but something hit him there, something hard. And he has a lot of smaller cuts, most of them on his hands, but nothing bad. His back and shoulders are badly burnt by the sun, and he has lost a lot of water. He was very nearly dead when they found him. I think we can say he was in an accident of some kind.'

'I agree with you,' said the inspector. 'But where? I mean, look at his hands.'

The inspector took the man's left hand and looked at it.

'He's wearing two gold rings and a gold watch, all good expensive things. Also his hands, under the cuts, are soft. So I don't think he works much with his hands. I would say he's a businessman of some kind. And he's quite a rich man, too.'

'Perhaps he's somebody who works in Oman, for the government or an oil company. Or perhaps he is a visitor to this country, someone on holiday,' said the doctor.

'I agree,' said the inspector. 'And if he is, his name and

photograph will be somewhere in my office with his visa. That is a good place to start looking, anyway.'

He took a small camera from his bag and took a photograph of the man in the bed.

'Right,' said the inspector. 'I'll get to work. Let me know at once if he wakes up or says anything you can understand. I'll let you know his name as soon as I find it.'

*   *   *

'Mum?'

'Yes, Andy?'

'I'm hungry.'

'I know, Andy. I'm hungry too. But we haven't got much food and drink. You know we have to be strong and wait for someone to find us.'

'The sun's coming up. Soon it'll be really hot again, like yesterday.'

'Yes, we must stay under the plane, out of the sun . . .'

'How's your foot?'

'Not very good. If I don't move, it's not too bad. But it hurts a lot.'

'Mum! What's that smell?'

'Is it from the plane?'

'I don't know. I'll have a look.' Andy stood up and walked around the plane.

'Mum! Something's running out of the engine. It's running down the plane into the sand. Perhaps it's water.'

'Water? From the engine?'

'Yes . . . no, it's not water. It must be petrol.'

'Petrol? We can use it to make a fire at night. Can you put it in something? If a plane comes, we can light a fire.'

'We haven't got anything to put it in.'

'Get the suitcases out of the plane. Take out the clothes and put one of them under the petrol. We can burn the clothes.'

'Burn our clothes?'

'Why not? We can buy new clothes. Our lives are more important than a few clothes. Put some of the clothes in the suitcase with the petrol.'

'OK, Mum, if you think so,' Andy replied.

'Yes. It's good to do something. It helps to give me hope. But what's happened to your father? I just hope he got to the coast all right.'

Chapter 7 *The man from nowhere*

Inspector Ibrahim went back to his office in Muscat. He looked at all the visas and all the photos of foreign men who were working in Oman. The man was not there. There was no news of a foreign man not at work or a foreigner on holiday not in his hotel. Everyone was there. But there was a man in the hospital without a name, a man who came from nowhere.

A police artist took the inspector's photo of the sleeping man and drew his eyes open on the picture.

That night, the photo of the man was on the Omani television news.

'Do you know this man?' asked the television news-reader. 'He was found on the east coast, north of Masirah Island three days ago. He is one metre 57 tall and weighs about 70 kilos. If you know his name or anything about him, please call any police station.'

They showed the picture on the Arabic news and the English news, but no-one called the police.

The next morning, Inspector Ibrahim came back to the hospital.

'Any news?' he asked Dr Singh. 'This is a bigger problem than I thought. I've sent this man's photo everywhere in the government, to every big business, and every large town in the country. I've even sent it to the other countries of the Gulf. I thought perhaps he works in the Gulf somewhere and came in by car on a visit here. But I've heard nothing from anyone. Nobody knows who this man is. He can't be working here or someone on holiday in this country. We'll have to start again and look at everything we know about him.'

Dr Singh looked at the man in the bed.

'Well, you know he has a cut on his head. It's quite deep, but clean. I think he hit his head on something hard. Or somebody hit him on the head with something hard. I know from his boots and his feet that he walked a long way, and he was badly burnt by the sun. So, I think we can say that he walked for a long time in the sun before he came to the beach. There was also some oil on his hands and on his trousers when he first arrived here. We washed and cleaned his head, arms and body. There was quite a lot of black oil on his hands, engine oil, I think.'

'So, perhaps he was in a car or a lorry,' said the inspector.

'Probably the engine stopped or he went off the road and hit something. That was when he hit his head. Then the car wouldn't go and he tried to mend the engine and got oil on his hands. But he couldn't mend it, so he walked a long way to get help. Perhaps he used his shirt to put round his head, and then lost it later.'

'It's possible, Inspector,' said the doctor. 'You could be right. But where was he going? There are no roads on the coast where they found him. Perhaps he was in a boat and its engine stopped. Perhaps he came to the beach and then walked along it, looking for a village. I can't believe he walked through the Wahiba Sands. You can't drive a car most places in the sands, not even a 4×4 drive. And nobody could go more than a few kilometres through the sands on foot.'

'A more important question,' said the inspector. 'Was he alone or were there other people with him? Are there people, perhaps hurt, waiting somewhere for help? I'm afraid we're not going to find the answers until this man wakes up. And then it may be too late.'

*   *   *

'Mum,' said Andy.

'Mmm?'

'Mum, I'm still cold.'

'Stay under my coat. It was a cold night, but now it's starting to get light again. When the sun comes up, it will be hot again.'

'Mum, the coat's all wet. Look, there's water on the coat.'

'Yes. It must be from the air, from the cold air.'

'Mum! Look! On the plane! On the wing of the plane! There's water everywhere. Look it's running down. It's water, clean water.'

'Quick. Get a handkerchief, no, get a clean shirt from a suitcase. Put it on the plane and wet it with the water. Then put the water in a cup, as much as you can. Oh, this is wonderful! Get as much of the water as you can before the sun comes up. As much as you can, Andy. Quickly. With this water we can be all right for another day or more.'

∗   ∗   ∗

The inspector left the hospital. The man slept all through that day and night. There was no news about him from anywhere.

Then the next morning the man woke up.

Chapter 8 *Awake*

It was the morning of the fourth day. The man opened his eyes and looked round the room. Imelda was sitting next to the bed.

The man looked at her, so she spoke to him. She spoke in English, and he answered her at once.

'Where am I?' he asked.

'You're in hospital,' said Imelda. 'In Muscat. You're OK. Everything is all right. Wait one moment and I'll get the doctor.'

Dr Singh came in quickly.

'Wonderful!' he said when he saw the man's eyes open. 'We are very happy to see you awake. Imelda, go and find Inspector Ibrahim at once and tell him the good news. He's somewhere in the hospital, I know. Try the main office. I'll have a talk with our friend here.'

He smiled at the man on the bed.

'You've been quite a problem for us, you know. Now then, can you tell me who you are and where you come from?'

'Yes, of course,' said the man. He started to speak, then he stopped. He looked at the doctor. Suddenly he looked afraid.

'I . . . I don't know,' he said. 'That's not possible. I can't remember. Oh, this is stupid. I can't even remember my name. This is terrible. What's wrong with me?'

'That's all right,' said the doctor. 'Take it easy. Don't be afraid. It often happens. You hurt your head. You've been in a coma, a deep sleep for three days. People often can't remember things at first. Just don't think about it. You'll soon remember things again.'

The man was hungry and thirsty. He drank a lot of water and ate some soup and fruit. Soon he looked much better. He was not so white. Imelda came in with Inspector Ibrahim and they sat by the bed and talked to the man.

'You were walking in the desert on the east coast,' said the inspector quietly. 'When people found you, you were on the beach, very ill. Do you know how you got there or what you were doing?'

The man was quiet for a few moments.

'It's no good,' he said. 'I have no idea. I can't even remember who I am.'

'It's all right,' said the inspector quickly. 'You're getting better all the time. You'll soon remember.'

'I feel so stupid,' said the man. 'Don't you know anything about me at all? What about my clothes, papers?'

'Nothing at all, I'm afraid,' said the inspector. 'Your clothes told us nothing.'

'You said something on the second morning,' said Imelda suddenly. 'You were asleep and it was only one or two words. But I think you said "red snow" and "Morphia". That's all.'

The man looked at Imelda. Suddenly he was very white.

'What . . . what was that?' he asked slowly.

'I think you said "Morphia" and then "red snow" when you were asleep,' said Imelda.

The man put his face in his hands.

'Oh my God!' he said. 'Morphia. Of course. Now I remember. Oh God! I can remember everything.'

The man lay back in the bed and put his hands over his face.

'How long have I been here?' he asked.

'Three and a half days,' said Dr Singh. 'It's almost four days since they found you on the beach.'

'What happened to my wife . . . my son?'

The inspector took the man's hand.

'Take it easy,' he said. 'You're still very weak. We'll help you if we can. But first we must know who you are and where you come from. Who are you? Do you know?'

'Yes. My name is Christos Bardis.'

The inspector's eyes opened wide.

'Not *the* Christos Bardis, of the Bardis Oil Tanker Company? The Greek millionaire?'

'Yes, that Christos Bardis. And my wife Morphia and my son Andreas were with me in the plane. We were flying back home from India . . .'

'Plane? What plane?' asked the inspector. 'You were lying on a beach on the east coast of Oman.'

'*My* plane, of course,' said Bardis. Now suddenly he was talking very quickly.

'Listen. There is a small plane, a Cessna, somewhere in the desert. It's all soft sand there.'

'Wahiba,' said the doctor. 'Oh my God! He crashed a plane in the Wahiba Sands.'

'We were coming home from a holiday in Bombay. I was flying north along the coast. We were going to Tehran. Then I saw the desert and I went down to show it to my

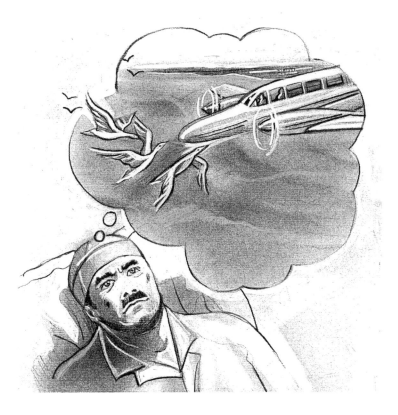

wife. A few minutes later the plane hit some birds. Something, perhaps a big piece of the window, hit me in the face. The plane was full of blood and bird feathers.

'I was quite badly hurt. I couldn't fly the plane. Morphia can't fly a plane. She tried, I remember, but it was no good. We came down in the desert, in the sand dunes.'

'But didn't you have a radio?' asked the inspector. 'Why didn't you call for help?'

'No time, I had no time. It all happened very quickly. When the plane hit the sand, it turned over. I hit my head on something and everything went black. My wife and my son Andy pulled me out of the plane. When I woke up, I was on the sand under one of the wings. My head hurt. There was blood everywhere, mostly bird's blood, not ours. I was very weak. But we were all alive.'

'And the radio was broken?' said the inspector.

'Yes, the front of the plane was all in pieces and half in a sand dune. Nothing worked.'

'So, what did you do?' asked the inspector.

'I had a quick look inside the plane. Everything was full of sand and there was oil everywhere. There was nothing I could do. Morphia put a shirt round the cut on my head, but I still had a really bad headache.'

'I believe you.' The doctor smiled. 'You hit your head very hard. You were lucky you didn't break it.'

'We had some water with us in the plane, some other drinks, and some food, some chocolate and biscuits. But not a lot, really. We had to choose. We could stay with the plane and wait for someone to find us, or we could try to find help, some people, a village. I didn't know where we were. We had no maps.

'Morphia wanted to stay by the plane. But no-one saw us crash. Nobody knew where we were because I changed our plans. I decided to fly to Bahrain, not Tehran. But I didn't have time to tell anyone. The plane crashed before I spoke to Bahrain. We are alone in the desert.

'I couldn't just sit and wait to die. I decided to go for help. I knew the sea was to the east. I thought it was very near, maybe about five kilometres. I decided to walk towards it.'

'Five kilometres in the Wahiba Sands are like twenty

34

kilometres anywhere else,' said the inspector. 'It's difficult to walk and it's very easy to go round and round in circles.'

'It was late in the afternoon,' said the man. 'I knew I had about three hours of light. And to go east I only had to keep the sun behind me. Anyway, I took some of the water with me, not a lot, and walked off towards the coast. I remember I finished the water after about an hour. I don't remember anything much after that. I was just walking and walking. The sand was soft and deep and the sun on my back was like a fire.'

The doctor spoke.

'You arrived at the sea at about six o'clock. You were badly burnt by the sun. What happened to your shirt?'

'I think I put it round my head and neck at some time. I had a terrible headache and my head felt very hot.'

'Well, you were lucky. You were near a small fishing village and some people found you and brought you to the hospital here in Muscat. But no-one has said anything about a plane.'

Bardis took the inspector's hand.

'They must still be there, in the desert, waiting. Please, Inspector, help me. We must find them. Money is not a problem, but we must find them as soon as possible.'

'Of course,' said the inspector. 'We'll start looking for the plane at once. And money is no problem, my friend. We will use every man and every helicopter we have. We'll find them.'

But Bardis did not answer. Suddenly, he was asleep again.

The inspector and the doctor left Imelda with him and

went out of the room. She heard the inspector say, 'Three or four days in the desert without food or water. It's a long time. What do you think?'

And the doctor answered, 'Not much hope, I'm afraid. They're probably already dead.'

Chapter 9   *Plans*

Ten minutes later in the next room, Inspector Ibrahim turned off his phone.

'All right,' he said to Dr Singh. 'There's a police helicopter at Sur. They will be in the air in about fifteen minutes.

'There's another police helicopter here in the capital city. The pilot will come here in about ten minutes and get me. Then there's the hospital helicopter. So that's three which can get to Wahiba before it's dark today. The others are all too far away, I'm afraid.'

'What shall we do there?' asked the doctor.

The inspector took a piece of paper and a pen.

'We'll make our plans in the air. We can all talk together on the radio. But look. Here is the coast to the east of Wahiba.'

He drew a line on the paper.

'And here is where they found Mr Bardis.'

He put a cross next to the line.

'Now we draw a line to the west. OK? How far did he walk? Ten kilometres? Let's say fifteen. He couldn't walk more than that.'

He drew another line on the paper.

'That's where the plane is, somewhere in there. I want you and the hospital helicopter to search the middle area, Area One. Three kilometres to the north and south of the

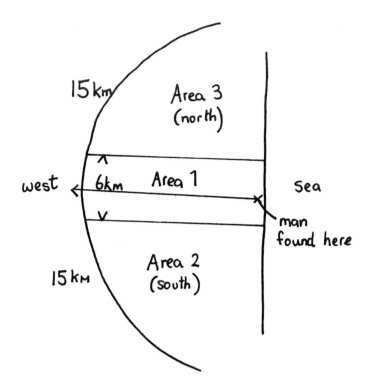

line. Tell your pilot to fly east and west, about half a kilometre more to the north each time.'

'OK,' said the doctor. 'And where will you be?'

'I'll take the area to the south, Area Two,' said the inspector. 'And the Sur helicopter will take the area to the north, Area Three. If we find them, we'll call you on the radio.'

They heard the noise of a helicopter outside the hospital.

'Time for me to go,' said the inspector.

'Good luck!' called the doctor as the inspector went out of the room.

'We'll need it!' called the inspector.

Suddenly there was a noise behind Dr Singh. He turned quickly. The door to Mr Bardis's room was open and Mr Bardis was standing there. He was wearing only a short hospital nightshirt. Behind him, Nurse Imelda was looking over his shoulder. Her face was very red.

'I'm sorry, doctor,' she called. 'I couldn't stop him.'

'Come on, Doctor,' said Bardis. 'Every minute is important. And I'm coming with you.'

'But Mr Bardis,' said Dr Singh, 'you're not well. You're still very weak.'

'You need every man you can get,' said Bardis, 'and I know my own plane. I'm coming with you. But first, will somebody please find me some trousers!'

Chapter 10   *The search*

At about four o'clock the three helicopters were near the Wahiba Sands. The inspector was talking to the pilots on the radio. Behind him was Bardis, his white face against the side window.

'We must search every metre of the sands to the west of where they found Mr Bardis,' the inspector was saying on the radio. 'We're looking for a small plane, a Cessna, which is down in the dunes. Perhaps it will be difficult to see. It could be half under the sand by now. The wind moves the sands all the time. Everybody has a map. The hospital helicopter will take the middle area; I'll go to the south and you, Abdullah, take the north. If you see anything, call at once on the radio and get the hospital helicopter there fast. We have about two or three hours before it is dark. There is a woman and a boy with the plane. We have to find them as soon as we can. Good luck.'

Late in the afternoon, the helicopters flew slowly over the red dunes of Wahiba. To the east and to the west they flew, following the lines on their maps. Eyes searched the red-gold sand until they hurt, looking for anything like a plane. Somewhere in the great sandy sea of Wahiba was a small plane and two people with it. They had to find them before the sun went down.

Two hours went by and the sun was low in the sky. Between the tops of the dunes, gold in the sun, it was a deep, dark purple. You could see almost nothing in it.

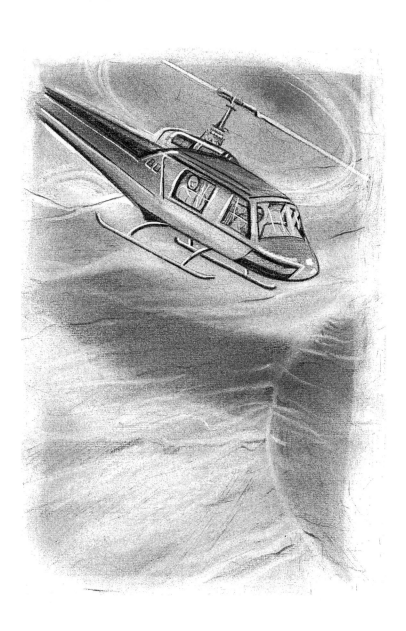

Inspector Ibrahim's eyes hurt.

'How long can we go on?' he asked the pilot. It was almost six o'clock and the sun was very low in the sky.

'We can search until it is too dark to see,' said the pilot. 'Then we must go back. We can't find them in the dark. We can start again first thing in the morning, of course, but by that time . . .'

'I know,' said the inspector, quietly. 'Another night in the desert. Another cold, dark night without food or water.'

He turned to Bardis. His white face was still against the window, his sad eyes looking deep into the dark dunes below.

'Are you OK, Mr Bardis?' asked the inspector. 'Perhaps you should rest your eyes for a few minutes.'

'I'm all right,' said Bardis. 'My head hurts, of course, and I'm feeling weak as a baby, but I can still see. How can I rest, even for a moment, when they are down there somewhere? We must keep looking, keep looking.'

'It's getting dark,' said the pilot quietly. 'Soon we'll have to stop looking and go back.'

'Give him a few more minutes,' said the inspector. 'We'll fly until it's all dark and we can't see anything.'

Chapter 11 *Fire in the desert*

'Mum! Mum! What's that noise?'

Andy pulled at his mother's arm, but she did not open her eyes. Her face was white and thin. She was in a deep sleep and he could not wake her up.

He looked up into the dark sky. He could hear an engine, a plane or a helicopter, somewhere in the dark sky above them.

'A fire!' he thought. 'I must make a fire.'

He took the cigarette lighter from his mother's bag and went to the suitcase. It was full of their clothes, all wet with petrol. He pulled it a little way away from the plane and looked at it.

'Careful,' he said. 'I must be careful. Petrol is dangerous. I mustn't get too near to it.'

The noise of the engine in the sky was far away now.

'Come on, come on!' he said to himself. He took a wet shirt from the suitcase and pulled it across the sand for a few metres. It left a wet line on the sand.

He took some pages from a magazine and held the lighter under them in his hand. Soon the paper was burning well.

He let the burning paper fall on the shirt. A line of fire ran across the sand and into the suitcase. There was a ball of fire and a strong hot wind. The suitcase was on fire.

Andy fell back into the sand. The clothes in the suitcase

were all burning now. The fire was getting bigger all the time.

'Yes!' he shouted. 'Yes! Go! Go! Go!'

The fire started to make a noise, a loud low noise. It ran across the sand to the plane. It began to run up the engine where it was deep in the sand.

'Oh no!' said Andy.

The fire went all round the engine and began to move along the wing and into the door of the plane.

Andy ran to his mother. She was lying a metre from the open door of the plane.

He shook her and shouted, but she did not move or wake up.

Andy put his hands under her arms and tried to pull her away from the burning plane. She was very heavy, too heavy. He could only move her a little. Each time he pulled her, she moved a few centimetres through the soft sand. But he was getting very tired now.

The fire was in the plane now, not just outside. The wing and one of the engines were burning too.

*   *   *

In the helicopter nobody was speaking. The light was all gone. Below them the desert was all black.

The pilot looked at the inspector.

'Yes,' he said. 'I think we must go back and start again first thing in the morning.'

The helicopter turned and moved north into the dark sky.

Behind the inspector, Bardis still sat with his sad white face against the glass.

Suddenly, he spoke.

'Wait! What's that? Over there.'

The pilot and the inspector looked to the left where Bardis was looking.

'It's a light,' said the pilot. 'A fire, I think.'

'A fire in the middle of the Wahiba Sands,' said the inspector. 'Let's see what it is, quickly.'

The helicopter moved fast to the left. The small light was soon bigger, a fire down in the dunes, a big fire.

'It's the plane!' shouted Bardis. 'I can see the plane. It's on fire down there.'

'He's right,' said the pilot. 'It's the plane, and it's burning. Wait just a moment. I'll put the helicopter down as near as I can.'

At that moment a ball of fire went up from the burning plane. For a few seconds the desert all around was as light as day.

'My God!' said the inspector. 'I hope the woman and the boy weren't near that.'

Chapter 12 *Dead or alive*

Inspector Ibrahim spoke to the helicopters in the search on the radio.

'This is Searcher One. This is Searcher One. We have found the plane. I say again. We have found the plane. It's on fire in the desert. We can't see any people. We are going down to look for them. I want the doctor and the hospital helicopter here as fast as possible.'

The police helicopter came down in the soft sand near the burning plane. The air was full of smoke from the burning plane and sand from the helicopter. All the desert was dark but around the burning plane it was as light as day.

The inspector and the pilot got out of the helicopter and started to run across the sand towards the crashed plane. In the back of the helicopter Bardis was still in his seat, weak, his head in his hands.

'Look,' said the pilot. 'Over there, near the plane. People.'

The inspector did not speak. He could see the two bodies lying together in the sand near the burning plane. They were not moving. He was afraid that they were too late.

The woman and the boy were lying close together. The woman was thin and white. There was sand in her long dark hair and her clothes. Her eyes were closed and her

face was very dry. The small boy was lying behind her, near her head. They did not move.

The inspector put his fingers on the woman's wrist, then on the side of her neck. For a few seconds no-one spoke.

'She's still alive,' said the inspector. 'By God! She's still alive. Quick, put some water on her face and mouth. I'll look at the boy.'

At that moment the boy turned his head and looked at them. He spoke weakly.

'Hello. Where have you been? We've been waiting for you for days and days. What did you think of my fire?'

The inspector smiled for the first time in many hours.

'It's a good one, Andy, a really good one. We could see it from miles away. Sorry we're late. We and your father had a few problems.'

The pilot was carefully washing the woman's face. He put a little water into her mouth and she moved her head a little.

'She's going to be all right, I think,' he said. 'Her foot is very bad, but she'll live. I'll get on the radio and tell the doctor to get here quickly.'

There was a loud noise from over their heads.

'No need for that.' The inspector smiled. 'Here comes the hospital helicopter now. Dr Singh will be with us in a few minutes.'

He turned to see the hospital helicopter come down. Mr Bardis was walking slowly and weakly across the sand. The inspector ran to help him. The boy saw him too and waved to him happily. And a few moments later the man from nowhere was back with his family.